This Fun Workbook Belongs To:

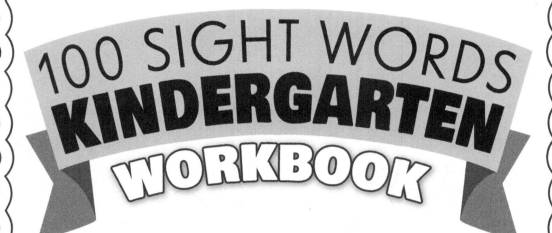

100 SIGHT WORDS KINDERGARTEN WORKBOOK

Lovingly Published by Big Dreams Art Supplies

Copyright © 2020 Big Dreams Art Supplies

BigDreamsArtSupplies.com

Illustrated by Davor Ratkovic

Printed in the United States of America

three

Trace the word and say it aloud!

three three three three

Write the word:

_____

_____

Complete the sentence with the word:

The mermaid can see [_ _ _ _ _] fish.

Grab a crayon and color the shapes with the word!

two three two seven six three three eight four five

four

Trace the word and say it aloud!

four four four four four

Write the word:

Complete the sentence with the word:

Find a [_ _ _ _] leaf clover.

Grab a crayon and color the shapes with the word!

five

Trace the word and say it aloud!

five five five five

Write the word:

Complete the sentence with the word:

There are ____ apples in a box.

three
five
five
five
five
two
one
six
six
four
five

Grab a crayon and color the shapes with the word!

six

Trace the word and say it aloud!

six ~six~ ~six~ ~six~ ~six~ ~six~ ~six~

Write the word:

Complete the sentence with the word:

The ice cream has [_ _ _] scoops.

Grab a crayon and color the shapes with the word!

one

six

three

four

six

six

two

six

six

five

seven

six

seven

Trace the word and say it aloud!

seven seven seven seven

Write the word:

Complete the sentence with the word:

I have [_____] balloons.

Grab a crayon and color the shapes with the word!

one
six
three
seven
seven
four
seven
seven
two
five
seven
seven

eight

Trace the word and say it aloud!

eight eight eight eight

Write the word:

Complete the sentence with the word:

An octopus has ⬚_____⬚ arms.

Grab a crayon and color the shapes with the word!

nine

Trace the word and say it aloud!

nine nine nine nine nine

Write the word:

Complete the sentence with the word:

Here are ____ flowers.

Grab a crayon and color the shapes with the word!

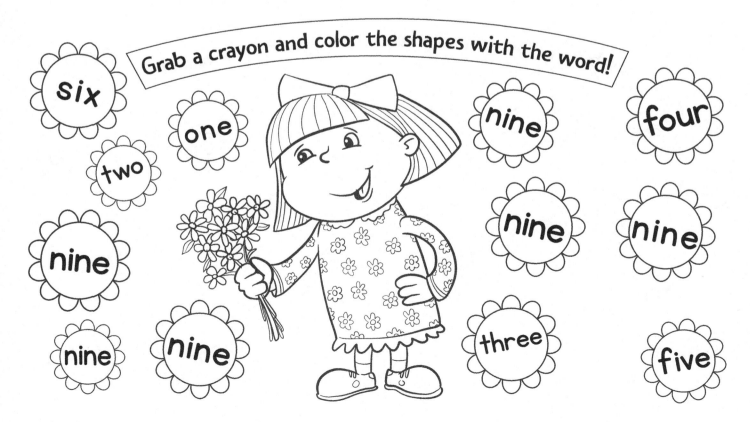

ten

Trace the word and say it aloud!

ten ten ten ten ten ten

Write the word:

_____

_____

Complete the sentence with the word:

I see [___] hearts.

three

ten

Grab a crayon and color the shapes with the word!

ten

two

six

ten

ten

ten

ten

one

four

five

black

Trace the word and say it aloud!

black black black black

Write the word:

_____

Complete the sentence with the word:

A [_ _ _ _ _] cat ran away.

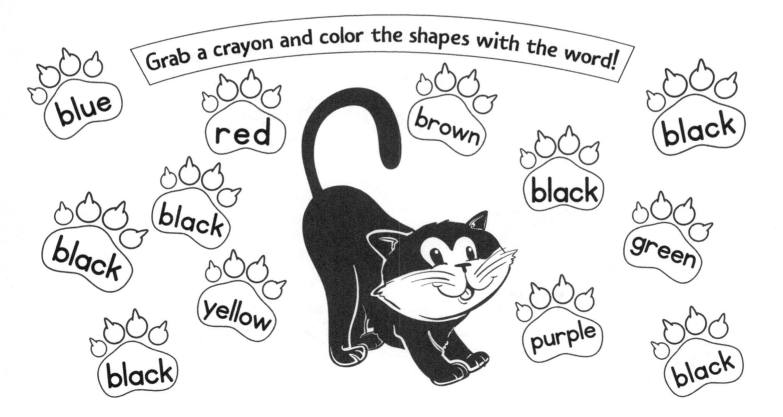

Grab a crayon and color the shapes with the word!

blue   red   brown   black
black   black   black   green
black   yellow   purple   black

blue

Trace the word and say it aloud!

blue blue blue blue

Write the word:

Complete the sentence with the word:

The bird is [_ _ _ _].

blue

Grab a crayon and color the shapes with the word!

brown   black   purple

blue   green   blue

red   blue

blue   yellow   blue

brown

Trace the word and say it aloud!

brown ....brown........ ....brown........

Write the word:

_____

_____

_____

Complete the sentence with the word:

Do you see a [_ _ _ _ _] dog?

Grab a crayon and color the shapes with the word!

white

brown

brown

blue

yellow

black

brown

brown

red

green

brown

brown

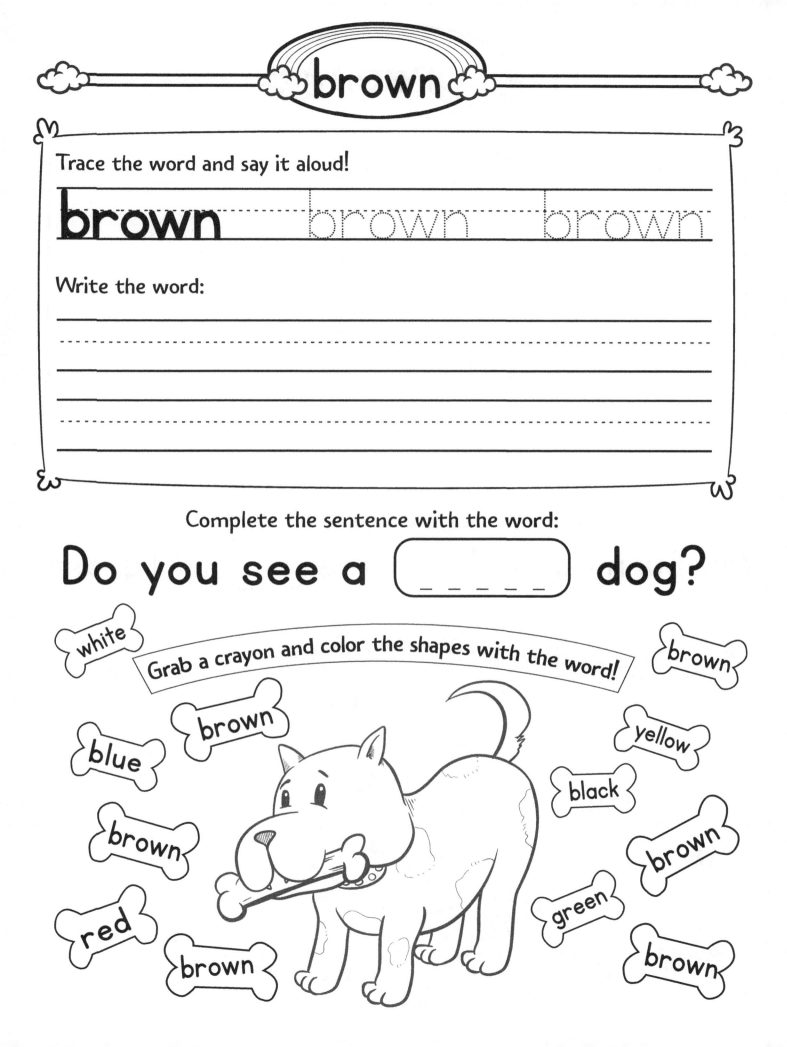

green

Trace the word and say it aloud!

green green green green

Write the word:

_____

_____

Complete the sentence with the word:

My bunny can play in the [_ _ _ _ _] grass.

Grab a crayon and color the shapes with the word!

brown   green

green   red

yellow

blue   green   purple

green   green   black   green

orange

Trace the word and say it aloud!

orange orange orange

Write the word:

Complete the sentence with the word:

The fox has [_____] fur.

Grab a crayon and color the shapes with the word!

yellow

orange

orange

black

orange

blue

red

green

orange

purple

orange

orange

pink

Trace the word and say it aloud!

pink pink pink pink pink

Write the word:

_____

- - - - - - - - - - - - - - - - -

_____

- - - - - - - - - - - - - - - - -

Complete the sentence with the word:

The princess has a [_ _ _ _] rose.

Grab a crayon and color the shapes with the word!

red

pink

black

pink

pink

blue

yellow

green

pink

purple

pink

pink

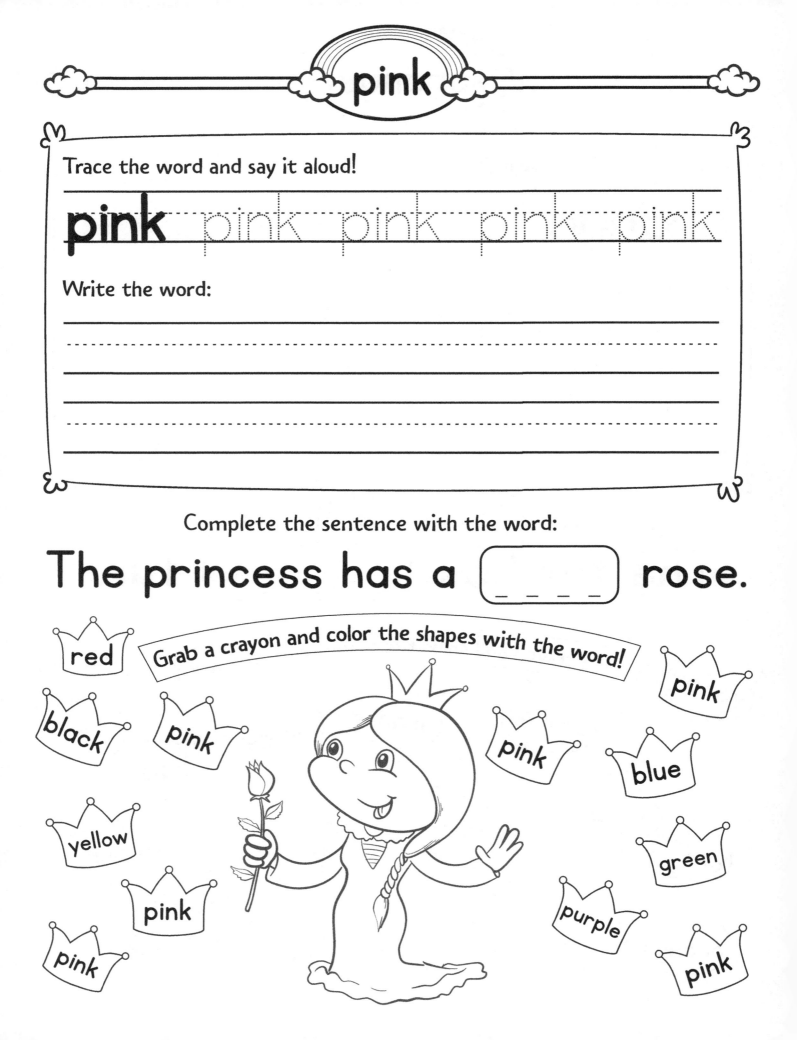

purple

Trace the word and say it aloud!

purple   purple   purple

Write the word:

Complete the sentence with the word:

My doll has a [_ _ _ _ _ _] dress.

Grab a crayon and color the shapes with the word!

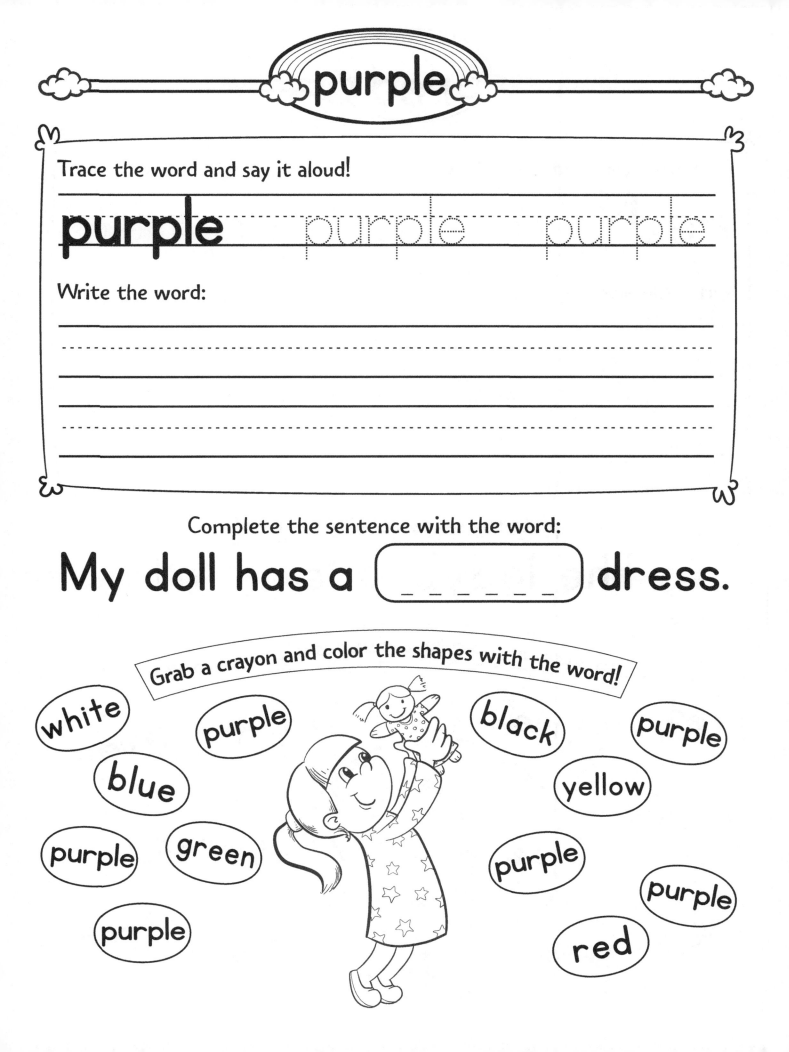

white purple black purple

blue yellow

purple green purple purple

purple red

red

Trace the word and say it aloud!

red red red red red

Write the word:

_____

- - - - - - - - - - - - - - - - - - - -

_____

_____

- - - - - - - - - - - - - - - - - - - -

_____

Complete the sentence with the word:

The ladybug is [_ _ _]

red

Grab a crayon and color the shapes with the word!

red   blue   purple   green

red   red

yellow   brown   black   red   red

yellow

Trace the word and say it aloud!

yellow   yellow   yellow

Write the word:

_____

_____

Complete the sentence with the word:

The sun is [_ _ _ _ _ _]

Grab a crayon and color the shapes with the word!

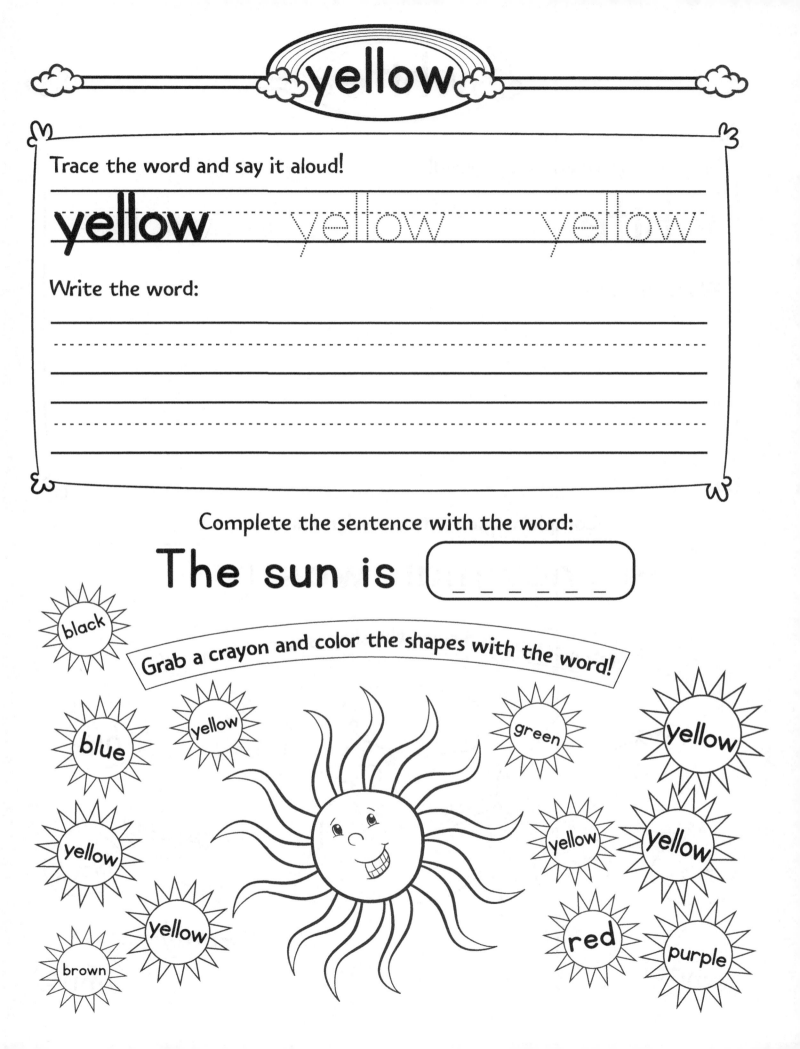

black · blue · yellow · green · yellow · yellow · yellow · yellow · red · purple · yellow · brown

white

Trace the word and say it aloud!

white white white white

Write the word:

Complete the sentence with the word:

The snowman was [_ _ _ _ _]

Grab a crayon and color the shapes with the word!

green

white

blue

white

white

white

red

black

brown

white

yellow

white

Trace the word and say it aloud!

a a a a a a a a a a

Write the word:

Complete the sentence with the word:

I see ⬚ mermaid tail.

Grab a crayon and color the shapes with the word!

a   are

all   a

a   am

at   a

a   a

an   and

all

Trace the word and say it aloud!

all all all all all all all

Write the word:

_____

- - - - - - - - - - - - - - - -

_____

- - - - - - - - - - - - - - - -

_____

Complete the sentence with the word:

I can read [_ _ _] the books.

Grab a crayon and color the shapes with the word!

an · all · am · all · all · all · are · and · all · a · at

Trace the word and say it aloud!

am am am am am am

Write the word:

Complete the sentence with the word:

I [_ _] smart!

all

am

Grab a crayon and color the shapes with the word!

am

are

am

am

a

an

am

at

am

and

an

Trace the word and say it aloud!

an an an an an an an

Write the word:

Complete the sentence with the word:

Get [__] umbrella if it is going to rain.

Grab a crayon and color the shapes with the word!

and

Trace the word and say it aloud!

and and and and and

Write the word:

_____

_____

_____

Complete the sentence with the word:

Dogs [_ _ _] cats like to play.

Grab a crayon and color the shapes with the word!

at

and

am

an

and

are

a

all

and

and

and

are

Trace the word and say it aloud!

are are are are are

Write the word:

Complete the sentence with the word:

Unicorns [_ _ _] pretty.

Grab a crayon and color the shapes with the word!

are
a
are
and
am
are

are
at
all
are
are
an

at

Trace the word and say it aloud!

at   at   at   at   at   at   at

Write the word:

Complete the sentence with the word:

You are good [_ _] this!

Grab a crayon and color the shapes with the word!

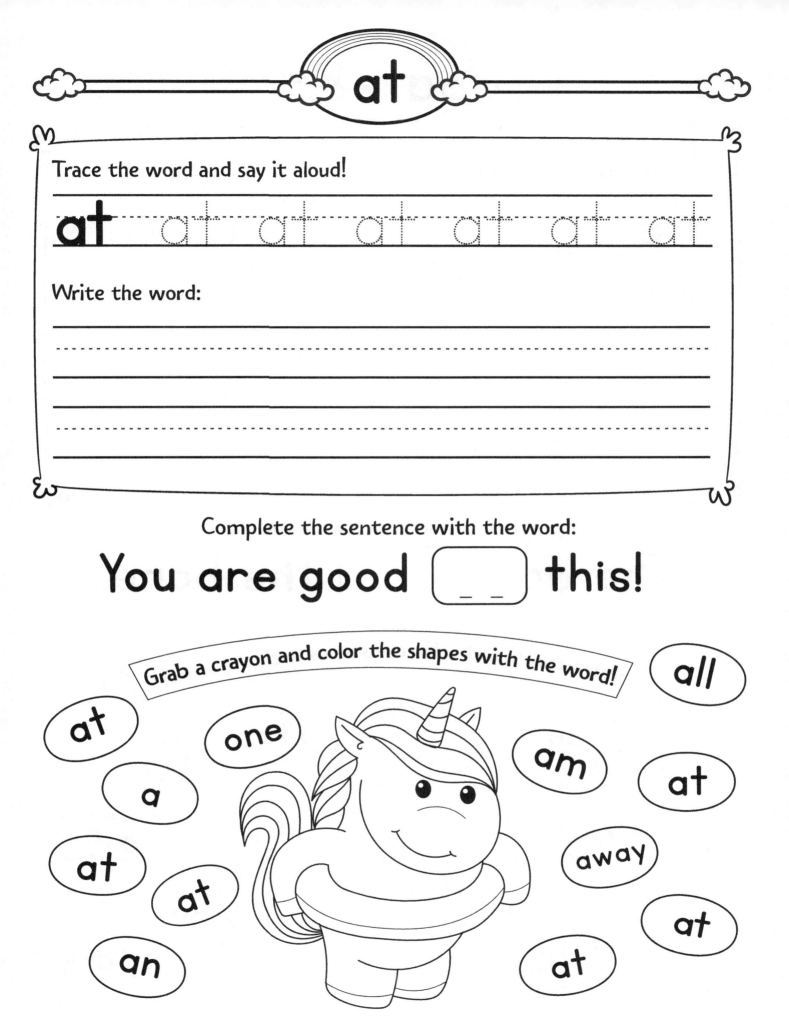

at   one   all   a   am   at   at   away   at   an   at   at

ate

Trace the word and say it aloud!

ate   ate   ate   ate   ate

Write the word:

Complete the sentence with the word:

The dog [_ _ _] the bone.

Grab a crayon and color the shapes with the word!

a   ate   ate   ate

ate   are

all   ate   ate

am   ate   an   and

away

Trace the word and say it aloud!

away away away away

Write the word:

Complete the sentence with the word:

The mermaid swam ____ .

am

at

Grab a crayon and color the shapes with the word!

away

away

away

are

away

away

and

away

an

all

be

Trace the word and say it aloud!

be be be be be be be

Write the word:

_____

_____

Complete the sentence with the word:

☐ the best you can!

Grab a crayon and color the shapes with the word!

be   boy   be   be

but   big

best   be   be   box

be   bad

big

Trace the word and say it aloud!

big big big big big big

Write the word:

_____

Complete the sentence with the word:

The queen lives in a [_ _ _] castle.

big Grab a crayon and color the shapes with the word! bus

but big bad big

be big big box

boy big

but

Trace the word and say it aloud!

but but but but but

Write the word:

_____

_____

_____

Complete the sentence with the word:

I like cake, [_ _ _] I like ice cream, too.

Grab a crayon and color the shapes with the word!

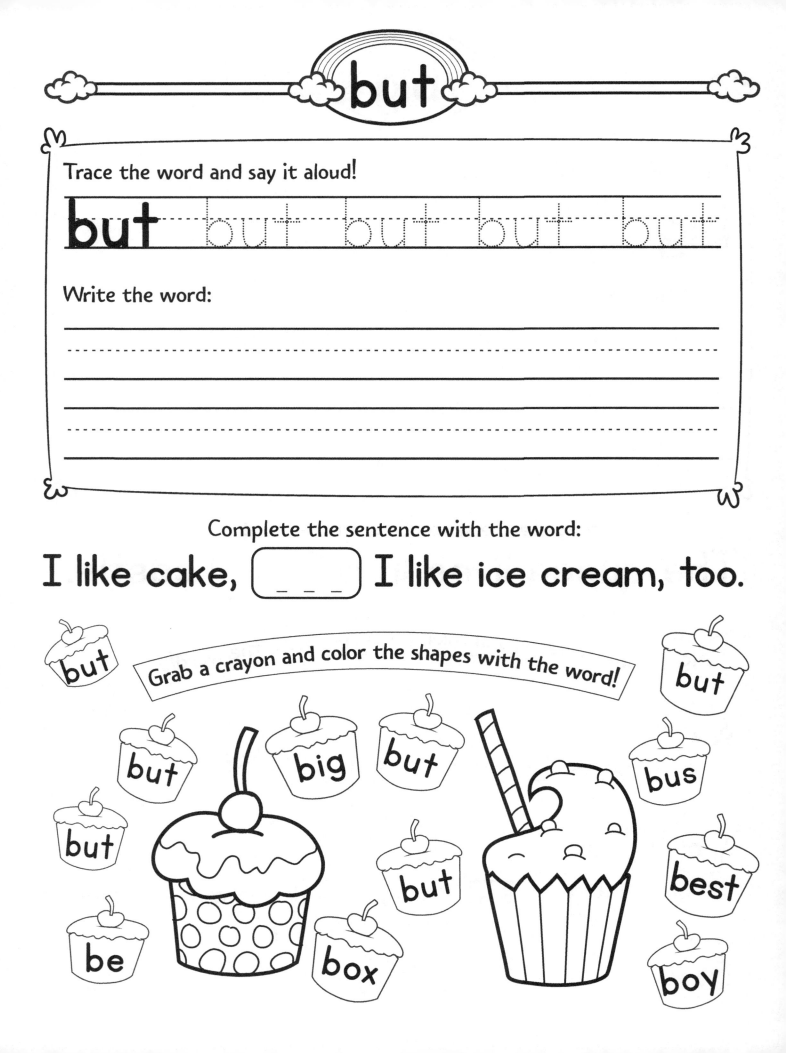

but · but · but · big · but · bus · but · but · best · be · box · boy

came

Trace the word and say it aloud!

came came came came

Write the word:

Complete the sentence with the word:

The birds [_ _ _ _] to the birdhouse.

car

Grab a crayon and color the shapes with the word!

came

came   cat   cup   came

came   came

cap

came   cut   can

can

Trace the word and say it aloud!

can can can can can

Write the word:

Complete the sentence with the word:

The fairy [_ _ _] fly fast.

Grab a crayon and color the shapes with the word!

can   cat
cap   can
car   came   can
cut   can   can   cup

do

Trace the word and say it aloud!

do do do do do do do do

Write the word:

Complete the sentence with the word:

[_ _] you like to dance?

Grab a crayon and color the shapes with the word!

dog

did

do

do

do

dad

day

do

dip

do

down

do

down

Trace the word and say it aloud!

down down down down

Write the word:

Complete the sentence with the word:

The fox runs [_ _ _ _] a hole.

Grab a crayon and color the shapes with the word!

dog   day   did   down

dip   down

down   dad

do   down   down   down

eat

Trace the word and say it aloud!

eat   eat   eat   eat   eat

Write the word:

_____

_____

Complete the sentence with the word:

What do you like to [_ _ _]?

every

eat

Grab a crayon and color the shapes with the word!

eat

ear

eat

end

eat

even

egg

eat

eye

eat

find

Trace the word and say it aloud!

find ┄find┄ ┄find┄ ┄find┄

Write the word:

Complete the sentence with the word:

Can you [_ _ _ _] a unicorn?

Grab a crayon and color the shapes with the word!

for

Trace the word and say it aloud!

for for for for for

Write the word:

Complete the sentence with the word:

The crown is [_ _ _] me.

for

Grab a crayon and color the shapes with the word!

fix

far

for

fan

for

for

for

fun

find

fly

for

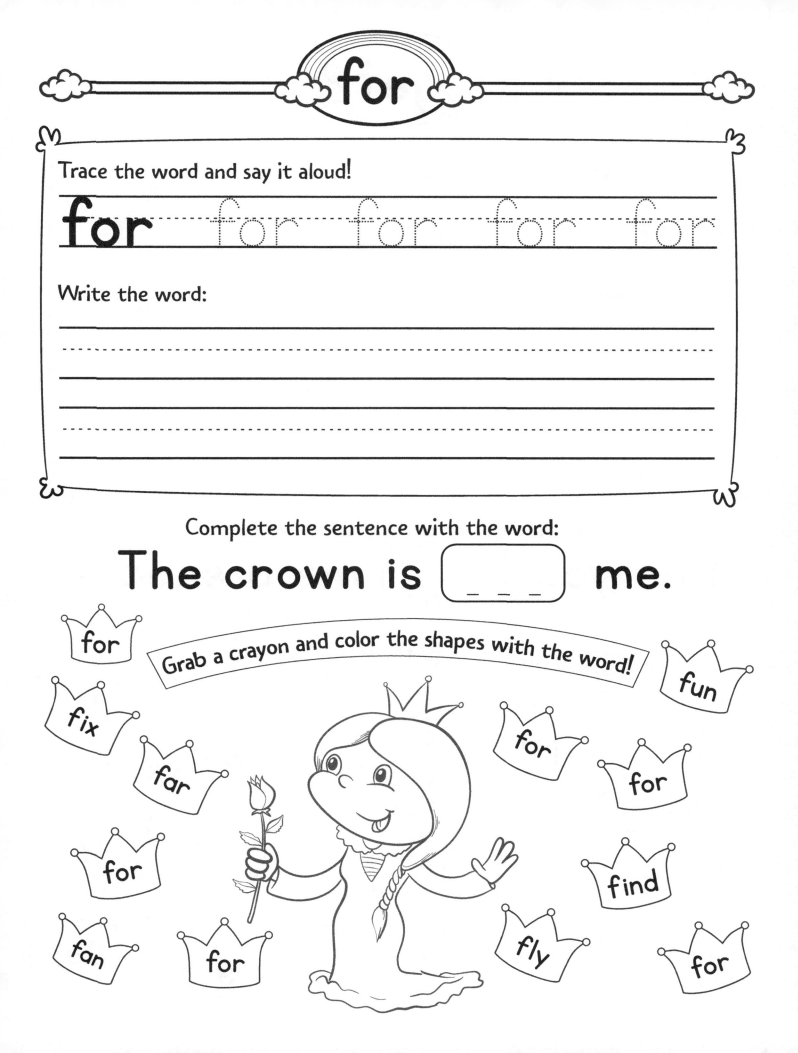

get

Trace the word and say it aloud!

get get get get get

Write the word:

_____

_____

Complete the sentence with the word:

Can you [_ _ _] me a snack?

Grab a crayon and color the shapes with the word!

go

gel

get

get

get

gap

get

gym

good

gem

get

get

get

go

Trace the word and say it aloud!

go go go go go go go

Write the word:

Complete the sentence with the word:

The horse can [_ _] fast.

Grab a crayon and color the shapes with the word!

gel
go
get
go
go
gem
gym
gap
go
good
go
go

good

Trace the word and say it aloud!

good good good good

Write the word:

Complete the sentence with the word:

The cupcake is [_ _ _ _] to eat.

Grab a crayon and color the shapes with the word!

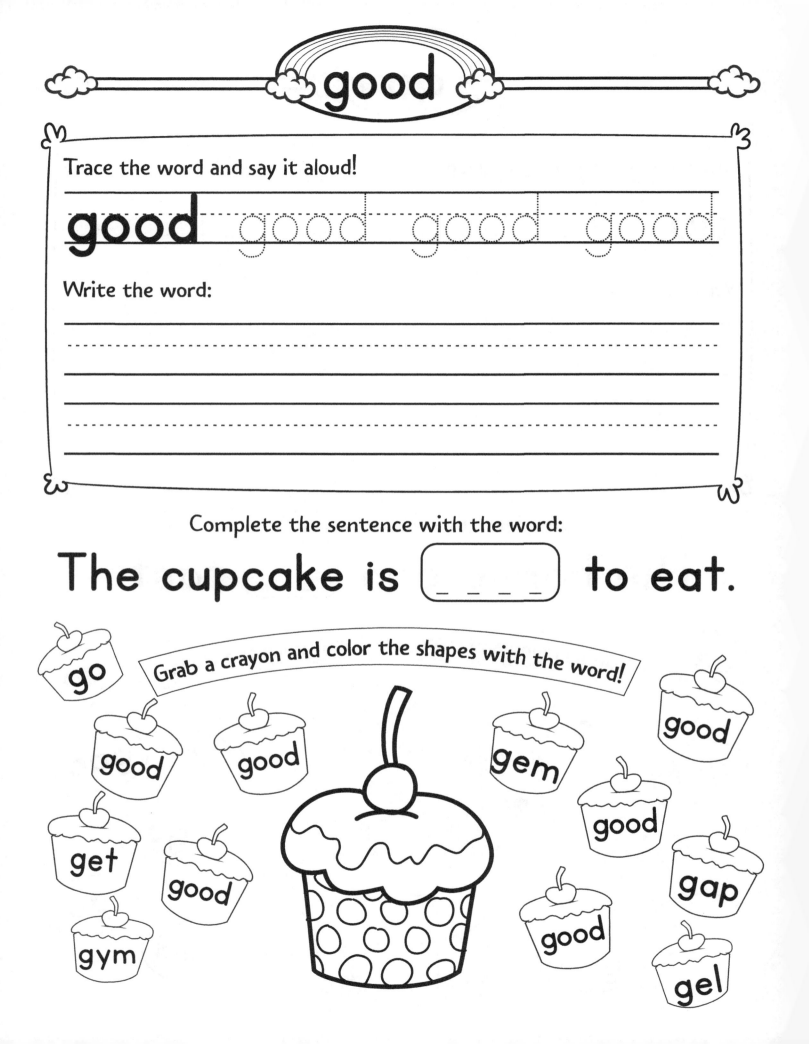

have

Trace the word and say it aloud!

have have have have

Write the word:

Complete the sentence with the word:

I [_ _ _ _] a kitten.

Grab a crayon and color the shapes with the word!

have

here

hat

have

help

have

had

have

hey

he

have

he

Trace the word and say it aloud!

he he he he he he he

Write the word:

Complete the sentence with the word:

 is my friend.

Grab a crayon and color the shapes with the word!

help

Trace the word and say it aloud!

help help help help help

Write the word:

Complete the sentence with the word:

I can [_ _ _ _] you.

Grab a crayon and color the shapes with the word!

have   help   here   help

had   hey

help   hat

he   help   help

help

here

Trace the word and say it aloud!

here here here here

Write the word:

Complete the sentence with the word:

| _ _ _ _ | is a treat!

Grab a crayon and color the shapes with the word!

I

Trace the word and say it aloud!

I

Write the word:

Complete the sentence with the word:

☐ like to play princess.

Grab a crayon and color the shapes with the word!

I is if it I I I I ice in I ink I

in

Trace the word and say it aloud!

in in in in in in in

Write the word:

Complete the sentence with the word:

I can ride [__] a carriage.

Grab a crayon and color the shapes with the word!

I

in   if   is   ink

in

in   in

ice   in   it

in   in

into

Trace the word and say it aloud!

into into into into into

Write the word:

_____

_____

Complete the sentence with the word:

I can go ⬚ the castle.

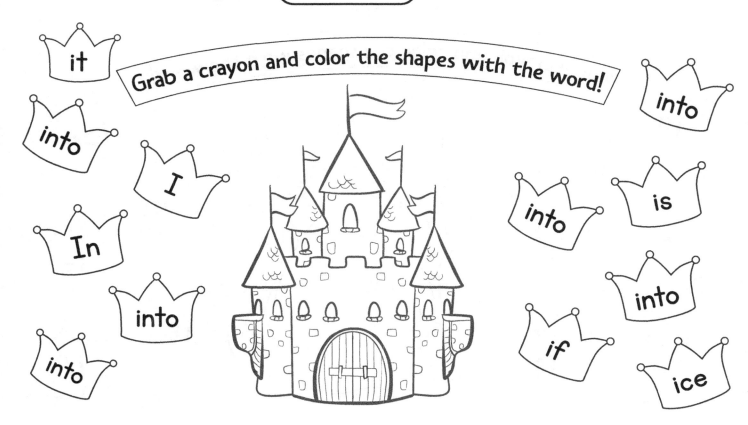

Grab a crayon and color the shapes with the word!

it · into · I · In · into · into

into · into · is · into · if · ice

is

Trace the word and say it aloud!

is is is is is is is

Write the word:

Complete the sentence with the word:

The unicorn ☐ my friend.

Grab a crayon and color the shapes with the word!

is   I   is   ice

it   is   in

into   is   is   is   if

it

Trace the word and say it aloud!

it it it it it it it it it

Write the word:

Complete the sentence with the word:

I can make [__] pretty.

in

it

if

Grab a crayon and color the shapes with the word!

it

is

ice

I

it

it

it

it

into

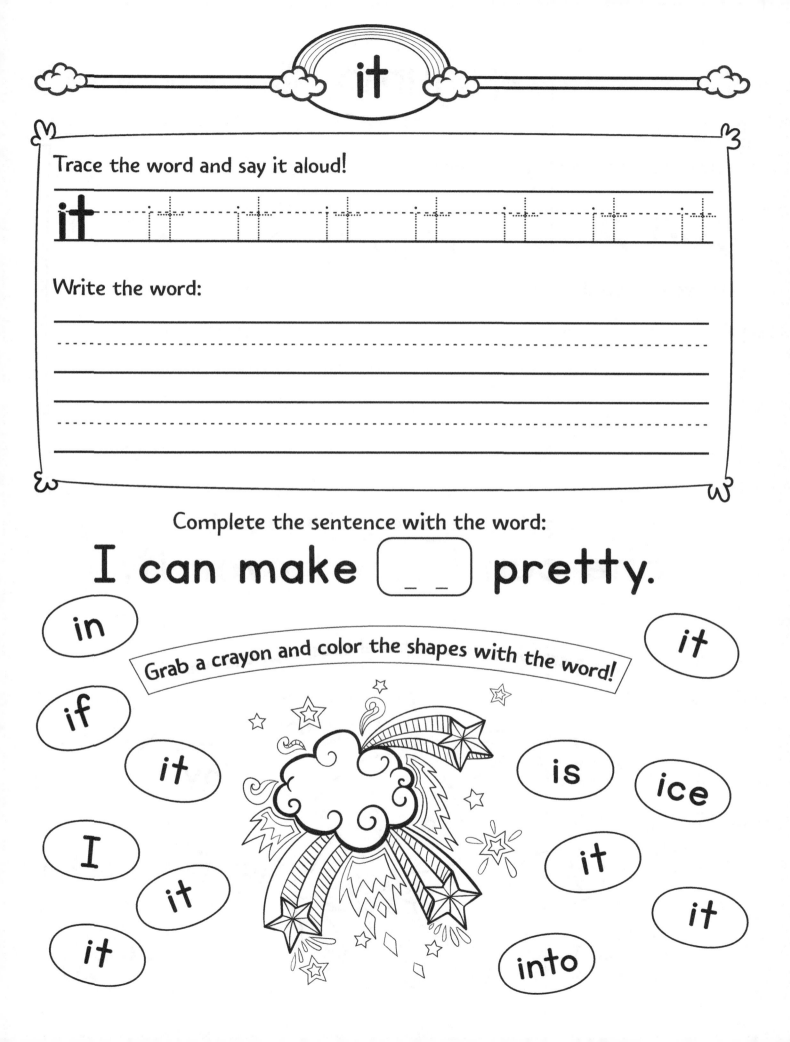

jump

Trace the word and say it aloud!

jump ⋯jump⋯ ⋯jump⋯ ⋯jump

Write the word:

Complete the sentence with the word:

She can [_ _ _ _] over it.

Grab a crayon and color the shapes with the word!

jump   job   jar   jump

joy

jump   jet   jump   jot

jam   jump   jump

like

Trace the word and say it aloud!

like ⠇⠊⠅⠑ ⠇⠊⠅⠑ ⠇⠊⠅⠑ ⠇⠊⠅⠑ ⠇⠊⠅⠑

Write the word:

Complete the sentence with the word:

I [_ _ _ _] you!

like   Grab a crayon and color the shapes with the word!   like

like   lot   like

lid

lay

little

like   leg   like   let

little

Trace the word and say it aloud!

little l̲i̲t̲t̲l̲e̲ l̲i̲t̲t̲l̲e̲ l̲i̲t̲t̲l̲e̲

Write the word:

_____

_____

Complete the sentence with the word:

The fairy is [_ _ _ _ _ _] .

Grab a crayon and color the shapes with the word!

like · little · leg · little · little · little · lid · little · lot · let · little · lay

look

Trace the word and say it aloud!

look look look look look

Write the word:

_____

- - - - - - - - - - - - - - - - - - - -

_____

- - - - - - - - - - - - - - - - - - - -

_____

Complete the sentence with the word:

[_ _ _ _] at this panda.

Grab a crayon and color the shapes with the word!

look
like
little look
lid
look

lot
let
look
look
look leg

make

Trace the word and say it aloud!

make ~~make make make~~

Write the word:

_____

Complete the sentence with the word:

I can [_ _ _ _] a cake.

Grab a crayon and color the shapes with the word!

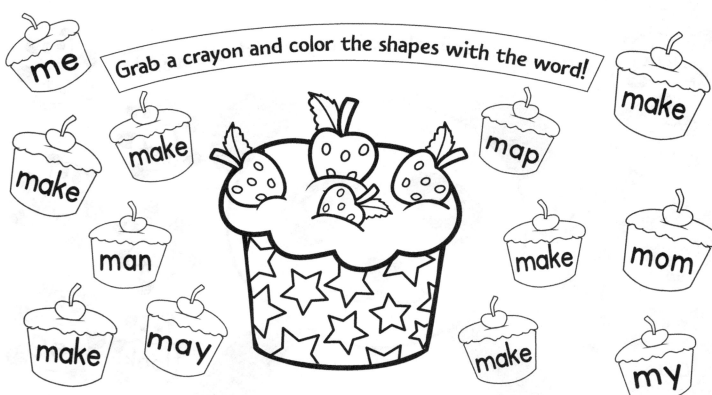

me

Trace the word and say it aloud!

me me me me me me

Write the word:

Complete the sentence with the word:

There is no one just like [__]!

mom

Grab a crayon and color the shapes with the word!

me

me

me

me

make

may

me

me

map

my

man

my

Trace the word and say it aloud!

my   my   my   my   my

Write the word:

Complete the sentence with the word:

[_ _] friend is happy.

Grab a crayon and color the shapes with the word!

my   mom   my   my   map

make   man

has   me   my

my   my

new

Trace the word and say it aloud!

new new new new new

Write the word:

_____

_____

Complete the sentence with the word:

I have a [_ _ _] toy.

Grab a crayon and color the shapes with the word!

nose

new

not

new

new

new

new

now

nap

no

net

new

no

Trace the word and say it aloud!

no no no no no no

Write the word:

Complete the sentence with the word:

___, you can not have that cookie.

Grab a crayon and color the shapes with the word!

no   net
new   no
not   no
no   nose
no no now no nap

not

Trace the word and say it aloud!

not not not not not not

Write the word:

Complete the sentence with the word:

I do [_ _ _] have the pretty necklace.

Grab a crayon and color the shapes with the word!

not not new not lot nap not no net not now

now

Trace the word and say it aloud!

now now now now now

Write the word:

Complete the sentence with the word:

I see a rainbow [_ _ _].

Grab a crayon and color the shapes with the word!

on

Trace the word and say it aloud!

on ͏on ͏on ͏on ͏on ͏on

Write the word:

Complete the sentence with the word:

There is a butterfly ☐ my finger.

Grab a crayon and color the shapes with the word!

our

Trace the word and say it aloud!

our our our our our

Write the word:

Complete the sentence with the word:

[_ _ _] garden has flowers.

Grab a crayon and color the shapes with the word!

our · out · our · our · one · on · okay · our · our · our · or · of

out

Trace the word and say it aloud!

out out out out out

Write the word:

Complete the sentence with the word:

Come [_ _ _] here and see the stars.

Grab a crayon and color the shapes with the word!

play

Trace the word and say it aloud!

play p̶l̶a̶y̶ p̶l̶a̶y̶ p̶l̶a̶y̶

Write the word:

Complete the sentence with the word:

Do you want to [_ _ _ _] with me?

Grab a crayon and color the shapes with the word!

pan play pot play play pin pie play play play put pet

please

Trace the word and say it aloud!

please   please   please

Write the word:

_____

_____

Complete the sentence with the word:

May I (_____) have a cookie?

Grab a crayon and color the shapes with the word!

please   pie

pan   please

pin   please   pot   please

put   please   pet   please

pretty

Trace the word and say it aloud!

pretty   pretty   pretty

Write the word:

_____

- -

_____

- -

_____

Complete the sentence with the word:

The mermaid has [_____] red hair.

Grab a crayon and color the shapes with the word!

put

pie

pretty

pretty

pan

pretty

pretty

pretty

pin

pot

pet

ran

Trace the word and say it aloud!

ran ran ran ran ran

Write the word:

Complete the sentence with the word:

The girl [_ _ _] fast.

Grab a crayon and color the shapes with the word!

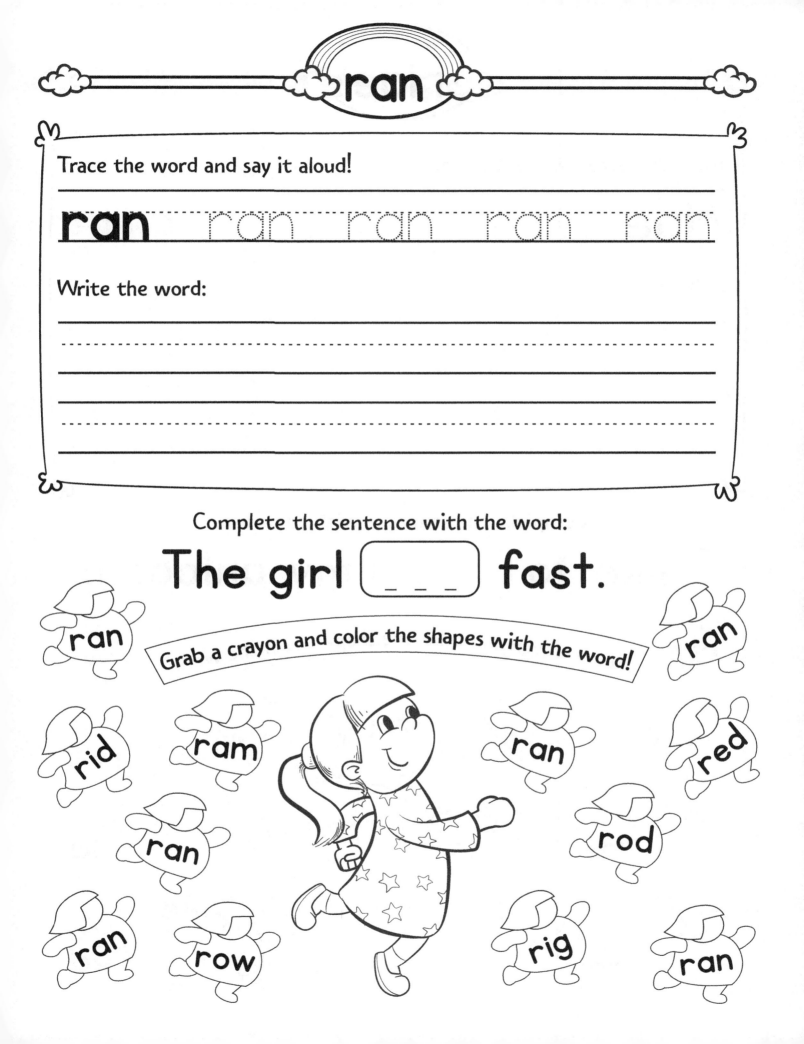

ran   ran

rid   ram   ran   red

ran   rod

ran   row   rig   ran

ride

Trace the word and say it aloud!

ride ride ride ride ride

Write the word:

_____

_____

Complete the sentence with the word:

I like to [_ _ _ _] my unicorn.

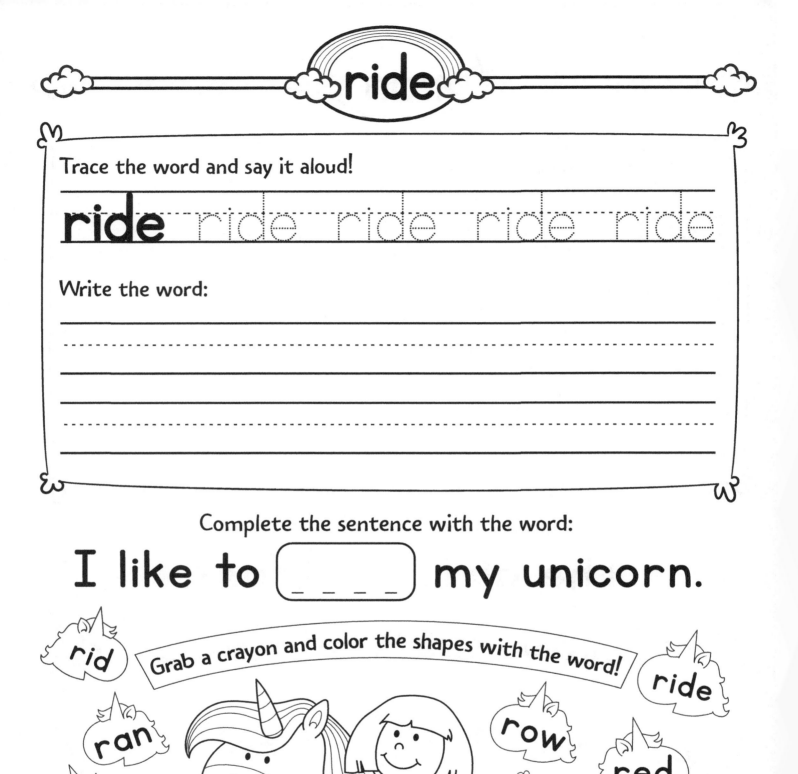

Grab a crayon and color the shapes with the word!

rid

ride

ran

row

red

ride

ride

ride

ride

ride

ram

rod

run

Trace the word and say it aloud!

run   run   run   run   run

Write the word:

Complete the sentence with the word:

I want to [_ _ _] in the sun.

Grab a crayon and color the shapes with the word!

run   run   red   ride   run   run   ran   ram   rid   rod   run

said

Trace the word and say it aloud!

said said said said

Write the word:

_____

- - - - - - - - - - - - - -

_____

- - - - - - - - - - - - - -

_____

Complete the sentence with the word:

The teacher [_ _ _] I can do it.

Grab a crayon and color the shapes with the word!

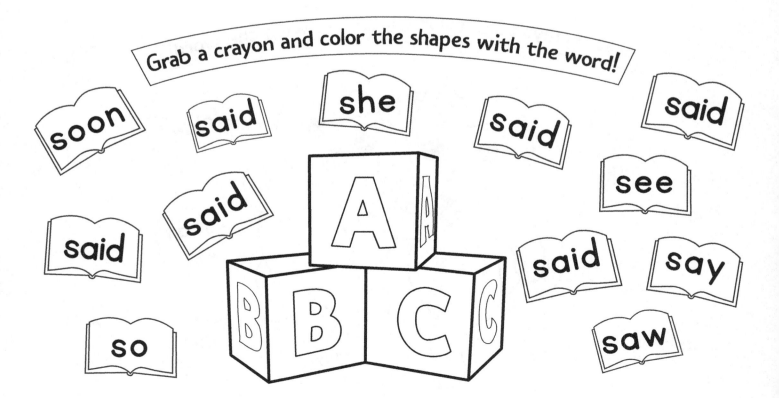

saw

Trace the word and say it aloud!

saw saw saw saw saw

Write the word:

Complete the sentence with the word:

She [_ _ _] an owl in a tree.

Grab a crayon and color the shapes with the word!

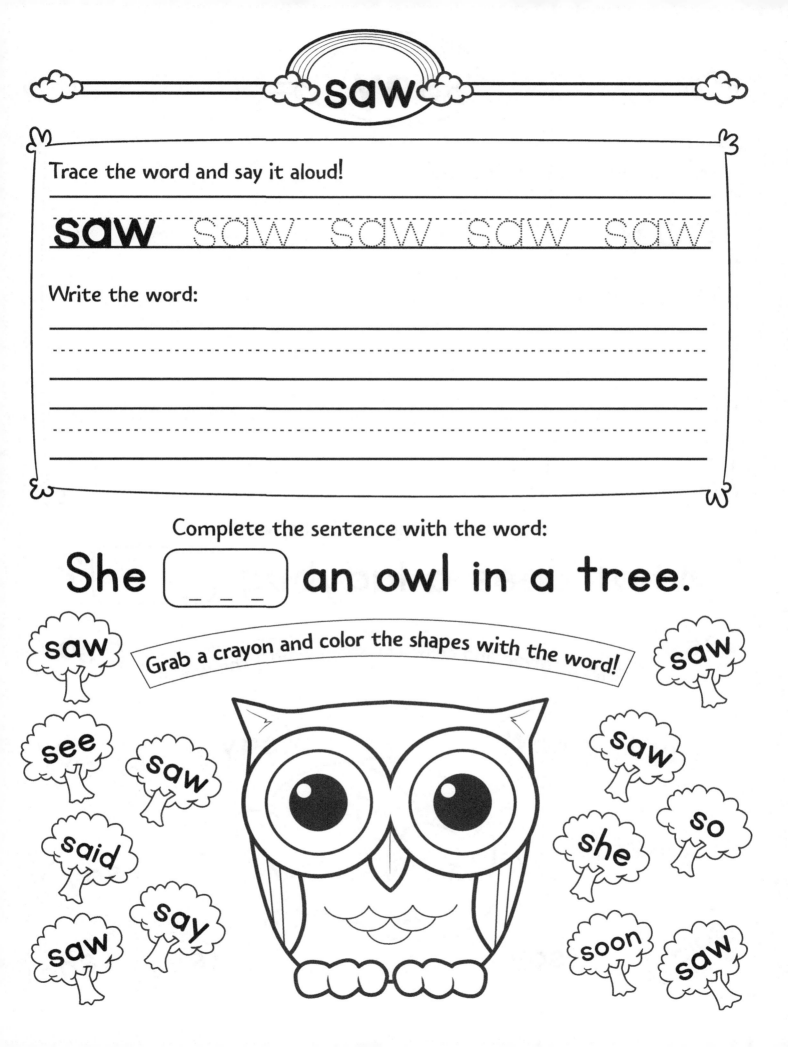

say

Trace the word and say it aloud!

say ˙say˙ ˙say˙ ˙say˙ ˙say˙

Write the word:

Complete the sentence with the word:

What does a ladybug ⬚___?

Grab a crayon and color the shapes with the word!

see

so

say

saw

say

soon

say

say

said

say

say

she

see

Trace the word and say it aloud!

see see see see see

Write the word:

Complete the sentence with the word:

I [____] a fairy.

see

see

Grab a crayon and color the shapes with the word!

say

saw

she

see

soon

so

said

see

see

she

Trace the word and say it aloud!

she she she she she

Write the word:

_____

_____

Complete the sentence with the word:

[___] **is a pretty singer.**

Grab a crayon and color the shapes with the word!

say

she

she

said

so

she

she

she

she

see

soon

she

saw

SO

Trace the word and say it aloud!

SO SO SO SO SO SO

Write the word:

Complete the sentence with the word:

Come outside ☐ we can play.

Grab a crayon and color the shapes with the word!

so | she | so | said | see | so | say | soon | so | saw | so

soon

Trace the word and say it aloud!

soon soon soon soon

Write the word:

Complete the sentence with the word:

The stars will be out ____.

soon

Grab a crayon and color the shapes with the word!

soon

soon

soon

see

saw

she

said

soon

soon

say

so

soon

that

Trace the word and say it aloud!

that that that that

Write the word:

_____

- - - - - - - - - - - - - - - -

_____

_____

- - - - - - - - - - - - - - - -

_____

Complete the sentence with the word:

The kitten is in ☐___☐ box.

that

this

Grab a crayon and color the shapes with the word!

they

that

there

that

to

that

that

the

try

that

the

Trace the word and say it aloud!

the the the the the

Write the word:

_____

_____

Complete the sentence with the word:

[____] rainbow is pink and purple.

Grab a crayon and color the shapes with the word!

to

the

this

the

the

try

that

the

there

they

the

the

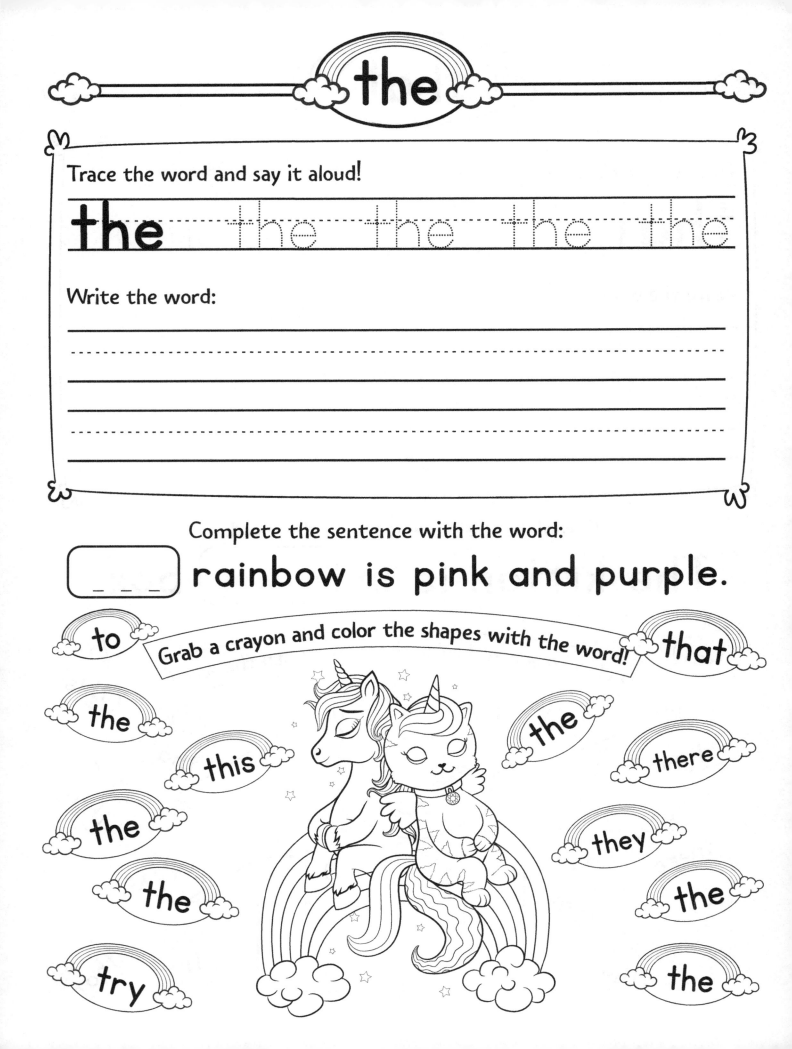

there

Trace the word and say it aloud!

there there there there

Write the word:

_____

Complete the sentence with the word:

My cake is over [_ _ _ _ _].

Grab a crayon and color the shapes with the word!

the

try

there

they

to

there

there

there

that

there

this

they

Trace the word and say it aloud!

they they they they

Write the word:

Complete the sentence with the word:

[_ _ _ _] are good friends.

Grab a crayon and color the shapes with the word!

the
they
this
there
they
to
they
that
try
they
they
they

this

Trace the word and say it aloud!

this this this this

Write the word:

Complete the sentence with the word:

[_ _ _ _] butterfly is pretty.

this

there

this

that

the

this

Grab a crayon and color the shapes with the word!

this

to

this

try

they

this

to

Trace the word and say it aloud!

to   to   to   to   to   to   to

Write the word:

_____

_____

Complete the sentence with the word:

The bunny went [__] his home.

to   Grab a crayon and color the shapes with the word!   this

the   to   to   they

to   to

that

there   try   to

under

Trace the word and say it aloud!

under   under   under

Write the word:

_____

_____

Complete the sentence with the word:

We had a tea party (_ _ _ _ _) the table.

Grab a crayon and color the shapes with the word!

under   under
us   upon
under   usual
up   under
use   unity
under   under

up

Trace the word and say it aloud!

up up up up up up up

Write the word:

Complete the sentence with the word:

The bird is ☐ in the sky.

Grab a crayon and color the shapes with the word!

want

Trace the word and say it aloud!

want want want want

Write the word:

_____

Complete the sentence with the word:

I [____] to eat a lollipop.

want

what

Grab a crayon and color the shapes with the word!

want

was

want

we

well

want

want

who

went

want

was

Trace the word and say it aloud!

was was was was was

Write the word:

Complete the sentence with the word:

The dog ☐_ _ _☐ cute.

Grab a crayon and color the shapes with the word!

we

Trace the word and say it aloud!

we we we we we

Write the word:

Complete the sentence with the word:

`___` make good cupcakes.

Grab a crayon and color the shapes with the word!

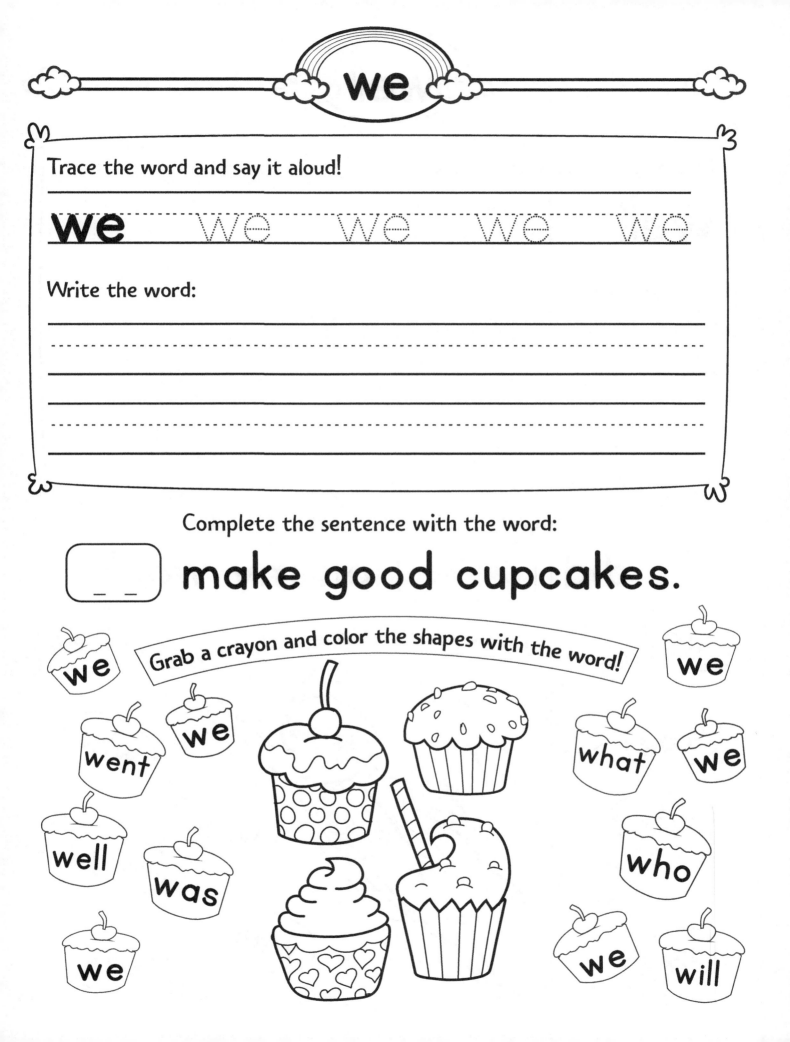

well

Trace the word and say it aloud!

well well well well well

Write the word:

_____

_____

Complete the sentence with the word:

I did [_ _ _ _] on my work.

Grab a crayon and color the shapes with the word!

we well well

was well who

what well

well will

well well with

went

Trace the word and say it aloud!

went ·went· ·went· ·went·

Write the word:

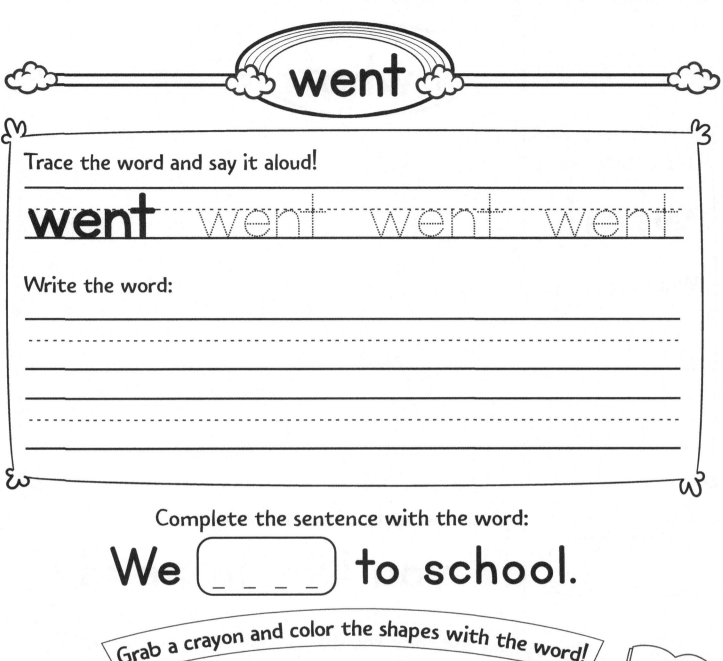

Complete the sentence with the word:

We [_ _ _ _] to school.

Grab a crayon and color the shapes with the word!

was   went   what   went
well   who
went   went   we   went   will   went

what

Trace the word and say it aloud!

what ·what· ·what· ·what·

Write the word:

Complete the sentence with the word:

_____ do you like to read?

Grab a crayon and color the shapes with the word!

we

what

what

well

what

went what

what

who

what

will

what

with

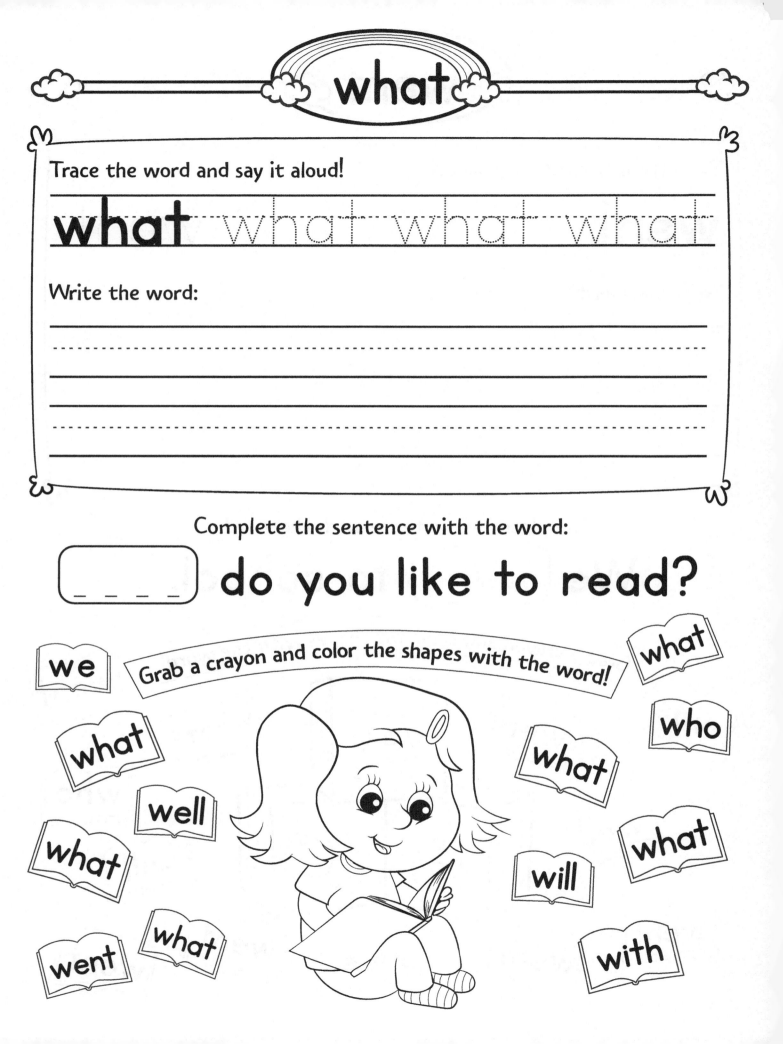

where

Trace the word and say it aloud!

where   where   where

Write the word:

Complete the sentence with the word:

[_____] is my crown?

Grab a crayon and color the shapes with the word!

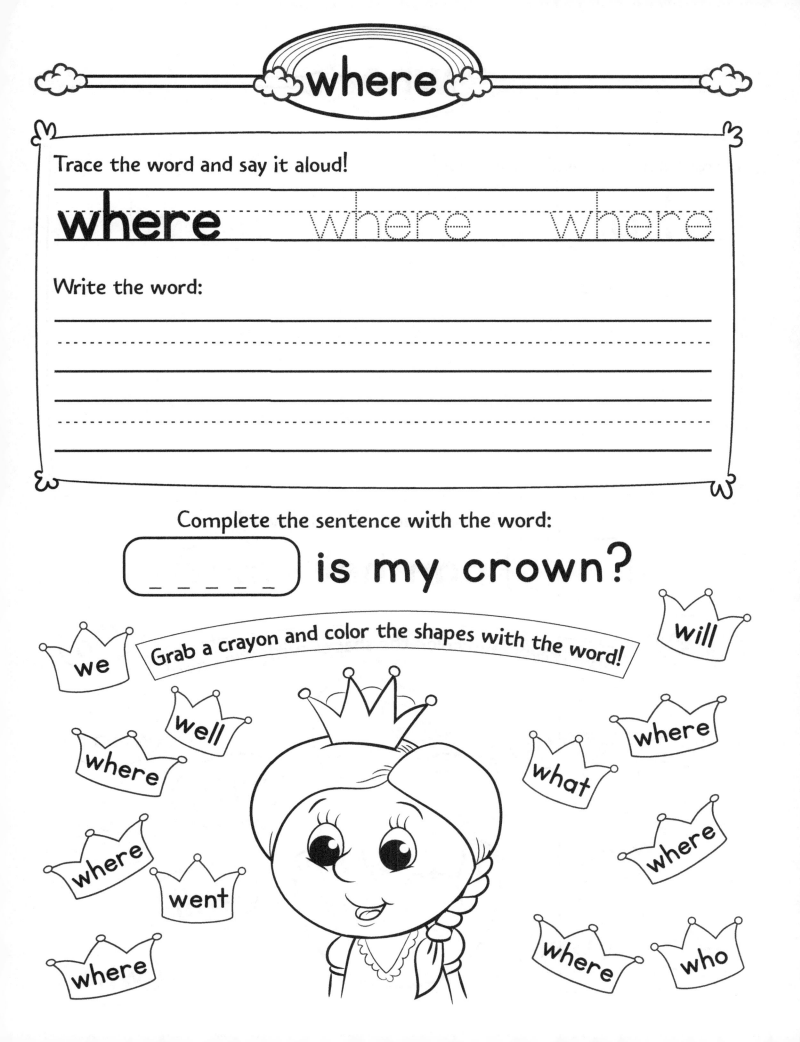

who

Trace the word and say it aloud!

who   who   who   who

Write the word:

_____

_____

Complete the sentence with the word:

[_ _ _] can help me?

Grab a crayon and color the shapes with the word!

we   who   who   what   with   who   went   will   who   well   who

will

Trace the word and say it aloud!

will will will will will will

Write the word:

_____

- -

_____

- -

_____

Complete the sentence with the word:

I [_ _ _ _] ride a brown horse.

Grab a crayon and color the shapes with the word!

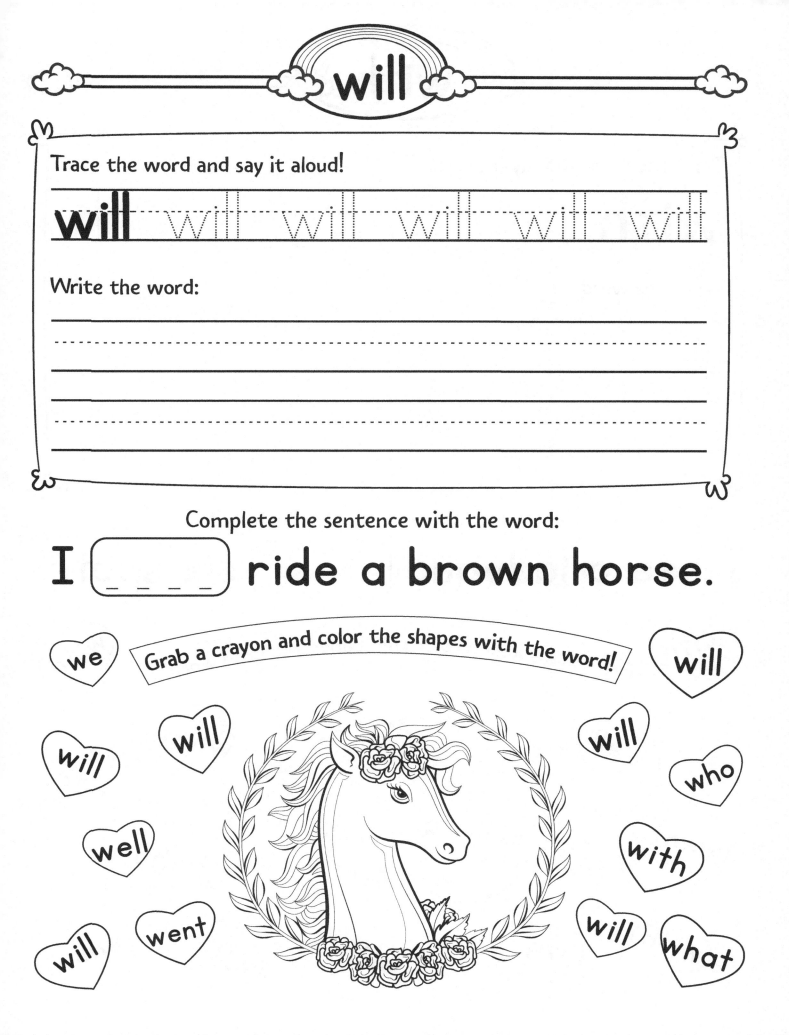

we

will

will

will

who

will

well

with

will

went

will

what

with

Trace the word and say it aloud!

with ....with........with........with

Write the word:

_____

- - - - - - - - - - - - - - - - - - -

_____

- - - - - - - - - - - - - - - - - - -

_____

Complete the sentence with the word:

I see a ladybug [____] six spots.

with

Grab a crayon and color the shapes with the word!

with

well

what

with

went

who

with

we

with

with

will

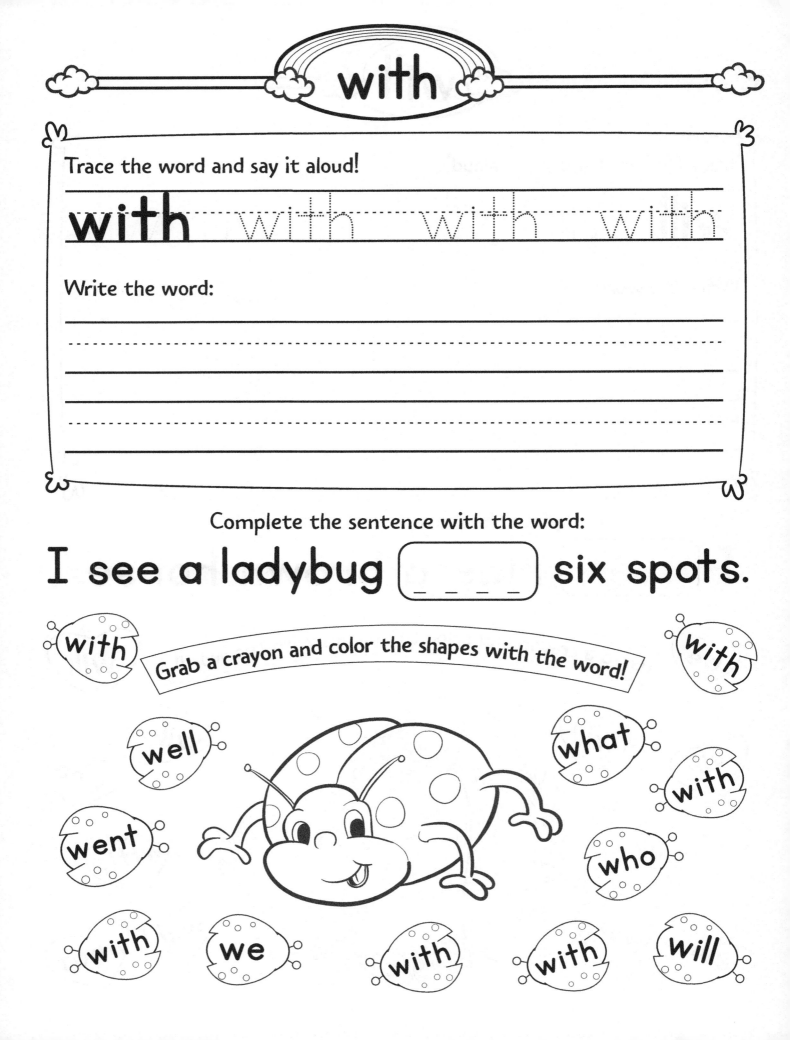

yes

Trace the word and say it aloud!

yes   yes   yes   yes   yes

Write the word:

Complete the sentence with the word:

[_ _ _], I can do this!

Grab a crayon and color the shapes with the word!

you

yes

yay

yard

year

yes

yam

yes

yes

yes

yeah

yes

you

Trace the word and say it aloud!

you　you　you　you　you

Write the word:

Complete the sentence with the word:

_ _ _ make me happy.

Grab a crayon and color the shapes with the word!

Cut Out These Flash Cards for More Practice Fun!

one	**two**
three	**four**
five	**red**
blue	**yellow**
green	**black**

six	seven
eight	nine
ten	white
brown	purple
pink	orange

seven

six

nine

eight

white

ten

purple

brown

orange

pink

a	all
am	an
and	are
at	ate
away	be

big	but
came	can
come	did
do	down
eat	find

for	get
go	good
have	he
help	here
I	in

into	is
it	jump
like	little
look	make
me	my

new	no
not	now
on	our
out	play
please	pretty

ran	ride
run	said
saw	say
see	she
so	soon

that	the
there	**they**
this	**to**
under	**up**
want	**was**

we	well
went	what
where	who
will	with
you	yes

well   we

what   went

who   where

with   war

we   war

Congratulations!

You are a

Sight Word Superstar!

You can read 100 sight words!

_____
Signature

_____
Date

Made in the USA
Monee, IL
30 March 2023

30915040R00070